THE NEW

FIRST MASS BOOK

An Easy Way of
Participating at Mass
for Boys and Girls

**With Official Text of People's Parts
of the Holy Mass
Printed in Bold Type**

In Accord with the Third Typical Edition
of the Roman Missal

D1855335

CATHOLIC BOOK PUBLISHING CORP.
NEW JERSEY

Dear Boys and Girls:

AT EVERY MASS we have God with us in a special way. We are with Jesus at the Last Supper, at his Passion and Death on the Cross, and at his Resurrection and Ascension. We are with him as he offers himself as a sacrifice to God our Father. We are with him as he comes to give us his Body and Blood at this special meal.

God is so good that he does not want us to wait until we see him in heaven before we eat at his table. He invites us to come now and eat the wonderful Bread of life, the Body and Blood of Jesus, which he prepares for us.

When we visit a friend for a meal, we usually bring him a little gift. At Mass, we bring bread and wine. God accepts this gift and makes it become the Body and Blood of Jesus who gives himself for us as a sacrifice to our Father.

This Mass Book will help you take a greater share in his holy Meal, by giving you the prayers recited at Mass and the Life of Jesus in pictures.

Nihil Obstat: Rev. James M. Cafone, M.A., S.T.D., Censor Librorum
Imprimatur: ✠ Most Rev. John J. Myers, D.D., J.C.D.,
Archbishop of Newark

(T-808)

Printed in China CPSIA September 2012 10 9 8 7 6 5 4 3 2 A/P

This Book Belongs to:

Who first became a child of God

and shared in His life on

Date of Baptism

Jesus came to me as food for my soul,

in the form of Bread,

for the first time on

Date of First Holy Communion

God gave me His Holy Spirit

to help me follow Jesus on

Date of Confirmation

At the Last Supper Jesus said:
"Do this in memory of me."

HOLY MASS

ON CALVARY Christ offered his Body and Blood to God the Father for us. In the Mass this great act is repeated.

Mass begins with the *Introductory Rites.* We speak to God in acts of contrition, praise and petition.

Then follows the *Liturgy of the Word.* We listen to what God says to us in the Readings, the Gospel and the Homily.

The *Liturgy of the Eucharist* has three parts. (1) With the Priest we offer the bread and wine *(Preparation of the Gifts).* (2) At the consecration this bread and wine are changed into the Body and Blood of Christ *(Eucharistic Prayer).* (3) In Holy Communion we receive Christ whom we love *(Communion Rite).*

Mass ends with the blessing and the dismissal *(Concluding Rites).*

THE ENTRANCE CHANT

As the Priest and ministers are coming in to the altar, the people sing the Entrance Chant which begins the celebration of Mass.

THE ORDER OF MASS

THE INTRODUCTORY RITES

ENTRANCE CHANT STAND

All make the Sign of the Cross:

PRIEST: In the name of the Father, and of the Son, and of the Holy Spirit.

PEOPLE: **Amen.**

THE GREETING

One of the following forms is used:
(Shown by A, B, or C)

A

PRIEST: The grace of our Lord Jesus Christ,
and the love of God,
and the communion of the Holy Spirit be with you all.

PEOPLE: **And with your spirit.**

B — OR —

PRIEST: Grace to you and peace from God our Father
and the Lord Jesus Christ.

PEOPLE: **And with your spirit.**

C — OR —

PRIEST: The Lord be with you.

PEOPLE: **And with your spirit.**

THE PENITENTIAL ACT

The people are invited to be sorry for their sins.

PRIEST: Brethren (brothers and sisters),
let us acknowledge our sins,
and so prepare ourselves to celebrate
the sacred mysteries.

Then one of the following forms is used.

A

PRIEST and **PEOPLE:**

I confess to almighty God
and to you, my brothers and sisters,
that I have greatly sinned,
in my thoughts and in my words,
in what I have done and in what I have failed to do,

And, striking their breast, they say:

through my fault, through my fault,
through my most grievous fault;

Then they continue:

therefore I ask blessed Mary ever-Virgin,
all the Angels and Saints,
and you, my brothers and sisters,
to pray for me to the Lord our God.

B —— OR ——

PRIEST: Have mercy on us, O Lord.

PEOPLE: **For we have sinned against you.**

PRIEST: Show us, O Lord, your mercy.

PEOPLE: **And grant us your salvation.**

C —— OR ——

PRIEST or other minister:
You were sent to heal the contrite of heart:
Lord, have mercy.

PEOPLE: **Lord, have mercy.**

PRIEST or other minister:
You came to call sinners:
Christ, have mercy.

PEOPLE: **Christ, have mercy.**

PRIEST or other minister:
You are seated at the right hand of the Father to intercede for us:
Lord, have mercy.

PEOPLE: **Lord, have mercy.**

Other invocations may be used.

At the end of any of the forms of the Penitential Act:

PRIEST: May almighty God have mercy on us,
forgive us our sins,
and bring us to everlasting life.

PEOPLE: **Amen.**

THE KYRIE

Unless it is included in the Penitential Act, the Kyrie is sung or said by the people with the choir, or cantor.

℣. Lord, have mercy.
℟. **Lord, have mercy.**
℣. Christ, have mercy.
℟. **Christ, have mercy.**
℣. Lord, have mercy.
℟. **Lord, have mercy.**

THE GLORIA

When the Gloria is sung or said the Priest or the cantor or everyone together may begin it:

Glory to God in the highest,
and on earth peace to people of good will.

We praise you,
we bless you,
we adore you,
we glorify you,
we give you thanks for your great glory,
Lord God, heavenly King,
O God, almighty Father.

Lord Jesus Christ, Only Begotten Son,
Lord God, Lamb of God, Son of the Father,
you take away the sins of the world,
have mercy on us;
you take away the sins of the world,
receive our prayer;
you are seated at the right hand of the Father,
have mercy on us.

For you alone are the Holy One,
you alone are the Lord,
you alone are the Most High,
Jesus Christ,
with the Holy Spirit,
in the glory of God the Father.
Amen.

THE COLLECT

The Priest prays in the name of all who are present. He asks God for the graces we need.

THE COLLECT

PRIEST: Let us pray.

Priest and people pray silently for a while.

Then the Priest says the Collect, which gives the theme of the particular celebration and asks God to help us.

Then he says:

Through our Lord Jesus Christ, your Son,
who lives and reigns with you in the unity of the Holy Spirit,
one God, for ever and ever.

PEOPLE: **Amen.**

The Liturgy of the WORD

THE FIRST READING

SIT

God Speaks to Us through the Prophets

We sit and listen to the word of God as it was spoken through his prophets and apostles. The reader takes their place in speaking to us.

At the end of the reading:

READER: The word of the Lord.

PEOPLE: **Thanks be to God.**

RESPONSORIAL PSALM

The people repeat the response sung by the cantor the first time and then after each verse.

THE SECOND READING

God Speaks to Us through the Apostles

At the end of the reading:

READER: The word of the Lord.

PEOPLE: **Thanks be to God.**

Jesus will speak to us in the Gospel. We rise now out of respect and prepare for his message with the Alleluia.

ALLELUIA

STAND

The people repeat the Alleluia after the cantor's Alleluia and then after the verse. During Lent one of the following invocations is used as a response instead of the Alleluia:

(1) **Glory and praise to you, Lord Jesus Christ!**
(2) **Glory to you, Lord Jesus Christ, Wisdom of God the Father!**
(3) **Glory to you, Word of God, Lord Jesus Christ!**
(4) **Glory to you, Lord Jesus Christ, Son of the Living God!**
(5) **Praise and honor to you, Lord Jesus Christ!**
(6) **Praise to you, Lord Jesus Christ, King of endless glory!**
(7) **Marvelous and great are your works, O Lord!**
(8) **Salvation, glory, and power to the Lord Jesus Christ!**

THE GOSPEL

God Speaks to Us through Christ

The Priest reads the Gospel in the name of Jesus, and Jesus himself becomes present among us through his word.

DEACON (or Priest):
The Lord be with you.

PEOPLE: **And with your spirit.**

DEACON (or Priest):

A reading from the holy Gospel according to N.

PEOPLE: **Glory to you, O Lord.**

We listen to the Priest or Deacon read the word of God.

At the end:

DEACON (or Priest):

The Gospel of the Lord.

PEOPLE: **Praise to you, Lord Jesus Christ.**

THE HOMILY

SIT

God Speaks to Us through the Priest

The Homily helps us to put the words of Christ into practice.

THE PROFESSION OF FAITH

I Believe All That I Have Heard

THE NICENE CREED **STAND**

I believe in one God,
the Father almighty,
maker of heaven and earth,
of all things visible and invisible.

I believe in one Lord Jesus Christ,
the Only Begotten Son of God,
born of the Father before all ages.
God from God, Light from Light,
true God from true God,
begotten, not made, consubstantial with the Father;
through him all things were made.
For us men and for our salvation
he came down from heaven,
and by the Holy Spirit was incarnate of the Virgin Mary, } bow
and became man.

For our sake he was crucified under Pontius Pilate,
he suffered death and was buried,
and rose again on the third day
in accordance with the Scriptures.
He ascended into heaven
and is seated at the right hand of the Father.

He will come again in glory
to judge the living and the dead
and his kingdom will have no end.

I believe in the Holy Spirit, the Lord, the giver of life,
who proceeds from the Father and the Son,
who with the Father and the Son is adored and glorified,
who has spoken through the prophets.

I believe in one, holy, catholic and apostolic Church.
I confess one Baptism for the forgiveness of sins
and I look forward to the resurrection of the dead
and the life of the world to come. Amen.

OR — THE APOSTLES' CREED

In celebrations of Masses with Children, the Apostles' Creed may be said after the Homily.

I believe in God,
the Father almighty,
Creator of heaven and earth,
and in Jesus Christ, his only Son, our Lord,
who was conceived by the Holy Spirit,
born of the Virgin Mary, } bow
suffered under Pontius Pilate,

was crucified, died and was buried;
he descended into hell;
on the third day he rose again from the dead;
he ascended into heaven,
and is seated at the right hand of God the Father almighty;
from there he will come to judge the living and the dead.

I believe in the Holy Spirit,
the holy catholic Church,
the communion of saints,
the forgiveness of sins,
the resurrection of the body,
and life everlasting. Amen.

THE UNIVERSAL PRAYER

(Prayer of the Faithful)

We Pray for Our Brothers and Sisters in Christ

After the Priest gives the introduction, the Deacon or other minister sings or says the invocations.

PEOPLE: **Lord, hear our prayer.**

(or other response, according to custom)

At the end the Priest says the concluding prayer:

PEOPLE: **Amen.**

OFFERTORY CHANT

SIT

THE PREPARATION OF THE GIFTS

While the gifts of the people are brought forward to the Priest and are placed on the altar, the Offertory Chant is sung.

THE PREPARATION OF THE GIFTS

The Priest thanks God for giving us the bread and wine that will be changed into Christ's Body and Blood. He says quietly:

Blessed are you, Lord God of all creation,
for through your goodness we have received
the bread we offer you:
fruit of the earth and work of human hands,
it will become for us the bread of life.

If there is no singing, the Priest may say this prayer aloud, and the people reply:

PEOPLE: **Blessed be God for ever.**

Preparation of the Wine

When he pours wine and a little water into the chalice, the Deacon (or the Priest) says quietly:

By the mystery of this water and wine
may we come to share in the divinity of Christ
who humbled himself to share in our humanity.

Before placing the chalice on the altar, the Priest says quietly:

Blessed are you, Lord God of all creation,
for through your goodness we have received
the wine we offer you:
fruit of the vine and work of human hands,
it will become our spiritual drink.

If there is no singing, the Priest may say this prayer aloud, and the people reply:

PEOPLE: **Blessed be God for ever.**

INVITATION TO PRAYER

PRIEST: Pray, brethren (brothers and sisters),
that my sacrifice and yours
may be acceptable to God,
the almighty Father.

PEOPLE: **May the Lord accept the sacrifice at your hands**
for the praise and glory of his name,
for our good
and the good of all his holy Church.

PRAYER OVER THE OFFERINGS

STAND

We Ask God to Accept Our Offerings

At the end:

PEOPLE: **Amen.**

EUCHARISTIC PRAYER

EUCHARISTIC PRAYER II

INTRODUCTORY DIALOGUE

PRIEST: The Lord be with you.

PEOPLE: And with your spirit.

PRIEST: Lift up your hearts.

PEOPLE: We lift them up to the Lord.

PRIEST: Let us give thanks to the Lord our God.

PEOPLE: It is right and just.

THE PREFACE

Our Prayer of Thanksgiving

Praise to the Father

It is truly right and just, our duty and our salvation,
always and everywhere to give you thanks, Father most holy,
through your beloved Son, Jesus Christ,
your Word through whom you made all things,
whom you sent as our Savior and Redeemer,
incarnate by the Holy Spirit and born of the Virgin.

THE SANCTUS

The Priest and people unite with the choirs of angels to praise God the Father, and Jesus whom he has sent.

Fulfilling your will and gaining for you
a holy people,
he stretched out his hands as he
endured his Passion,
so as to break the bonds of death and
manifest the resurrection.

And so, with the Angels and all the
Saints
we declare your glory,
as with one voice we acclaim:

THE SANCTUS

First Acclamation of the People

PRIEST and **PEOPLE:**

Holy, Holy, Holy Lord God of hosts.

Heaven and earth are full of your glory.

Hosanna in the highest.

Blessed is he who comes in the name of the Lord.

Hosanna in the highest.

KNEEL

Invocation of the Holy Spirit

You are indeed Holy, O Lord,
the fount of all holiness.
Make holy, therefore, these gifts, we pray,
by sending down your Spirit upon them like the dewfall,
so that they may become for us
the Body and ✠ Blood of our Lord Jesus Christ.

The Lord's Supper

At the time he was betrayed
and entered willingly into his Passion,
he took bread and, giving thanks, broke it,
and gave it to his disciples, saying:

Take this, all of you, and eat of it,
for this is my Body,
which will be given up for you.

ELEVATION OF THE HOST

The Priest shows the consecrated host to the people, places it again on the paten, and genuflects in adoration.

In a similar way, when supper was ended,
he took the chalice
and, once more giving thanks,
he gave it to his disciples, saying:

Take this, all of you, and drink from it,

for this is the chalice of my Blood,

the Blood of the new and eternal covenant,

which will be poured out for you and for many

for the forgiveness of sins.

Do this in memory of me.

ELEVATION OF THE CHALICE

The Priest shows the chalice to the people, places it on the corporal, and genuflects in adoration.

PRIEST: The mystery of faith.

PEOPLE:

**A We proclaim your Death, O Lord,
and profess your Resurrection
until you come again.**

— OR —

**B When we eat this Bread and drink this Cup,
we proclaim your Death, O Lord,
until you come again.**

— OR —

**C Save us, Savior of the world,
for by your Cross and Resurrection
you have set us free.**

The Memorial Prayer

Therefore, as we celebrate
the memorial of his Death and Resurrection,
we offer you, Lord,
the Bread of life and the Chalice of salvation,

giving thanks that you have held us worthy
to be in your presence and minister to you.

Invocation of the Holy Spirit

Humbly we pray
that, partaking of the Body and Blood of Christ,
we may be gathered into one by the Holy Spirit.

Intercessions: For the Church

Remember, Lord, your Church,
spread throughout the world,
and bring her to the fullness of charity,
together with N. our Pope and N. our Bishop
and all the clergy.

For the Dead

Remember also our brothers and sisters
who have fallen asleep in the hope of the resurrection,
and all who have died in your mercy:
welcome them into the light of your face.

In Communion with the Saints

Have mercy on us all, we pray,
that with the Blessed Virgin Mary, Mother of God,
with the blessed Apostles,
and all the Saints who have pleased you throughout the ages,
we may merit to be coheirs to eternal life,
and may praise and glorify you
through your Son, Jesus Christ.

Concluding Doxology

Through him, and with him, and in him,
O God, almighty Father,
in the unity of the Holy Spirit,
all glory and honor is yours,
for ever and ever.

PEOPLE: **Amen.**

AT THE END OF THE EUCHARISTIC PRAYER

At the end of the Eucharistic Prayer, lifting the host and chalice, the Priest gives honor and glory to God through Jesus. We join him as we acclaim: AMEN.

THE LORD'S PRAYER

Our preparation for very close union with Jesus in Holy Communion begins with the "Our Father," the prayer that Jesus taught us to say.

THE COMMUNION RITE

STAND

THE LORD'S PRAYER

PRIEST: At the Savior's command
and formed by divine teaching,
we dare to say:

(Other options may be used.)

PRIEST and **PEOPLE:**

Our Father, who art in heaven,
hallowed be thy name;
thy kingdom come,
thy will be done
on earth as it is in heaven.
Give us this day our daily bread,
and forgive us our trespasses,
as we forgive those who trespass against us;
and lead us not into temptation,
but deliver us from evil.

PRIEST: Deliver us, Lord, we pray, from every evil,
graciously grant peace in our days,

that, by the help of your mercy,
we may be always free from sin
and safe from all distress,
as we await the blessed hope
and the coming of our Savior, Jesus Christ.

PEOPLE: **For the kingdom,
the power and the glory are yours
now and for ever.**

SIGN OF PEACE

The Priest says the prayer for peace and concludes: for ever and ever.

PRIEST: For ever and ever.

PEOPLE: **Amen.**

PRIEST: The peace of the Lord be with you always.

PEOPLE: **And with your spirit.**

PRIEST: Let us offer each other the sign of peace.

The people exchange a sign that expresses peace, communion, and charity, in keeping with local customs.

BREAKING OF THE BREAD

The people sing or say:

Lamb of God, you take away the sins of the world,
have mercy on us.
Lamb of God, you take away the sins of the world,
have mercy on us.
Lamb of God, you take away the sins of the world,
grant us peace.

PRAYER BEFORE COMMUNION

We pray in silence and then voice words of humility and hope as our final preparation before meeting Christ in the Eucharist.

Before Communion, the Priest says quietly one of the following prayers:

Lord Jesus Christ, Son of the living God,
who, by the will of the Father
and the work of the Holy Spirit,
through your Death gave life to the world,
free me by this, your most holy Body and Blood,
from all my sins and from every evil;
keep me always faithful to your commandments,
and never let me be parted from you.

— OR —

May the receiving of your Body and Blood,
Lord Jesus Christ,
not bring me to judgment and condemnation,
but through your loving mercy
be for me protection in mind and body
and a healing remedy.

COMMUNION

PRIEST: Behold the Lamb of God,
behold him who takes away the sins of the world.
Blessed are those called to the supper of the Lamb.

PRIEST and **PEOPLE** (once only):
Lord, I am not worthy
that you should enter under my roof,
but only say the word
and my soul shall be healed.

The Priest then receives Communion.

COMMUNION OF THE PEOPLE

We offered Jesus to the Father. Now we receive Jesus in Holy Communion as God's gift to us.

COMMUNION OF THE PEOPLE

PRIEST: The Body of Christ.

COMMUNICANT: Amen.

PRIEST: The Blood of Christ.

COMMUNICANT: Amen.

COMMUNION CHANT

The Communion Chant is sung while Communion is given to the faithful.

SIT

PERIOD OF SILENCE OR SONG OF PRAISE

After Communion there may be a period of silence, or a song of praise may be sung.

PRAYER AFTER COMMUNION

PRIEST: Let us pray.

STAND

Priest and people may pray silently for a while. Then the Priest says the Prayer after Communion.

At the end:

PRIEST: Through Christ our Lord.

PEOPLE: Amen.

THE CONCLUDING RITES

We have heard God's word and eaten the Body of Christ. Now it is time for us to leave, to do good works, to praise and bless the Lord in our daily lives.

THE BLESSING

After any brief announcements (sit), the Blessing and Dismissal follow:

PRIEST: The Lord be with you.

PEOPLE: **And with your spirit.**

PRIEST: May almighty God bless you, the Father, and the Son, ✠ and the Holy Spirit.

PEOPLE: **Amen.**

DISMISSAL

DEACON (or Priest):

A Go forth, the Mass is ended.

B Go and announce the Gospel of the Lord.

C Go in peace, glorifying the Lord by your life.

D Go in peace.

PEOPLE: **Thanks be to God.**

The LIFE OF CHRIST IN PICTURES

✠

Each Sunday and feastday Mass contains parts that change in accord with the particular mystery of Christ's life. In this way, every year the prayers at Mass recall for us the Life, Death, Resurrection and Ascension of Jesus.

This section will help you to know our Lord's life better, so you can take a more active part at every Mass during the year.

✠

Jesus Is Born

THE BIRTH OF JESUS

THE Roman Emperor Augustus ordered all the people under his rule to be counted. Joseph and Mary left their home in Nazareth and traveled to Bethlehem.

So many people had come to be registered that there was no room for them in the inn. Outside the town, on the hills, they found a cave.

It was here that Jesus was born. Mary wrapped him in soft clothing and laid him in a manger.

Jesus was the Son of God. He came to help us on our way to the Father.

Jesus Speaks with the Learned Men

THE CHILD JESUS IN THE TEMPLE

WHEN Jesus was twelve years old, he went up to Jerusalem with Mary and Joseph. After the feast, his parents started home and discovered that Jesus was not with them.

For three days they looked for him without finding him.

At last they found Jesus in the Temple, surrounded by learned men, listening to them and asking them questions.

Mary did not understand that Jesus was doing the work of his Heavenly Father. He returned obediently to Nazareth.

John Baptizes Jesus in the Jordan

THE BAPTISM OF JESUS

WHEN Jesus was about thirty years old, it was time for him to go out and to preach the good news. He traveled down to the region around the Jordan River so that he could be baptized by John the Baptist.

When John had poured the water over Jesus' head, the skies above him opened up and the Spirit of the Lord descended upon him in the form of a dove. Then there was a voice that came from the heavens and said, "This is my beloved Son. My favor rests on him."

John was confused by Jesus' request, for he knew Jesus was much holier than he. But Jesus told John that this was the way it should be, for they were to fulfill God's commands.

THE WEDDING FEAST AT CANA

ONE day Mary went to a marriage feast in Cana with Jesus and his disciples.

At one point, Mary saw that there was not enough wine, so she told Jesus.

He ordered the waiters to fill six big water jars with water and to carry the water to the steward. When the steward tasted the water, it had become wine. This was Jesus' first miracle.

JESUS CURES A BLIND MAN

A BLIND man was brought to Jesus. He asked: "Lord, that I might see."

Jesus had pity on him and said: "Receive your sight. Your faith has saved you."

At once the man could see again. He went away praising God.

Jesus Teaches His Apostles

JESUS PREACHES LOVE FOR GOD AND NEIGHBOR

WHEN Jesus grew up, he went about preaching and doing good. He told the people that the Kingdom of God had come.

Jesus selected twelve Apostles to be his companions and helpers. Many other people also followed him.

Very often, these people gathered together to listen to Jesus' teaching. One day Jesus climbed up on a mountain and had the people sit down to listen to him.

He told the people to love God and do his will. He also told them to love their neighbor, and forgive one another.

Mary Listens to Jesus

JESUS WITH MARTHA AND MARY

JESUS often visited Martha, her sister Mary, and their brother Lazarus.

One day Mary sat at the feet of Jesus listening to him, while Martha rushed about preparing the meal.

Martha became annoyed and said, "Lord, is it no concern of yours that my sister has left me to serve alone? Tell her to help me."

Jesus replied, "Martha, Martha, you are anxious and troubled about many things; and yet only one thing is necessary. Mary has chosen the best part, and it will not be taken away from her."

Jesus Blesses the Children

JESUS LOVES CHILDREN

JESUS loved children and they loved him. One day some of the people brought their children to him so that he might bless them.

But the Apostles thought that the children should not bother Jesus, so they tried to keep the children away from him.

Our Lord noticed what they were doing and scolded them. He said to the Apostles: "Let the little children come to me, for the kingdom of God is made up of them."

And Jesus put his arms around the children and began to bless them.

Jesus Speaks about God the Father

JESUS SPEAKS ABOUT GOD THE FATHER

WHEN Jesus was living on earth, he often spoke to the disciples about his Father. He loves his Father, and he wants everyone to know that his Father is powerful and good.

The Father loves Jesus and sent him into the world to teach everyone how to pray and how to serve the Father.

Once, when the Apostles asked Jesus to teach them how to pray, he taught them a prayer that helps us to place our trust in God, our Father.

When we pray the *Our Father*, also called the *Lord's Prayer*, we are saying a prayer given to us directly by Jesus so many years ago.

JESUS RAISES JAIRUS'S DAUGHTER

THE daughter of the ruler Jairus had just died. But Jesus said to him, "Do not be afraid. Only have faith and she shall be saved."

As Jesus entered the house, all were weeping for her. He said, "Do not weep. She is asleep, not dead." Taking the girl by the hand, he cried out, "Girl, arise." And she stood up and began to walk.

THE MIRACLE OF THE LOAVES AND FISH

PEOPLE liked to listen to Jesus, and they did not want to leave him.

One day Jesus told the Apostles to give the crowd something to eat. The Apostles were worried. There were more than 5,000 hungry people. But all they had was a basket with five loaves and two fish. Jesus blessed this food and all had their fill.

Jesus Calls Peter "Rock"

JESUS NAMES PETER THE FIRST POPE

ONE day Jesus asked his disciples who they thought he was. Some said he was John the Baptist, or Elijah, or Jeremiah, or one of the prophets. It was Peter who stepped forward and said: "You are the Christ, the Son of the living God."

Jesus knew that no one of this earth had revealed this to Peter. The revelation could have come only from his heavenly Father. He then said to Peter: "I say to you, you are Peter, and upon this rock I will build my Church. And the gates of hell shall not prevail against it."

Peter was to be the shepherd of the Church, for he was to show it as much love as Jesus, the Good Shepherd, had shown to him and the other disciples.

Jesus, Moses, and Elijah
Appear in Glory

THE TRANSFIGURATION

ONE day Jesus took Peter, James, and John up to Mount Tabor to pray.

While Jesus was praying, his appearance suddenly changed. His face and clothes became white as wool, as bright as the sun. Suddenly the disciples saw that there were two men speaking to Jesus: Moses and Elijah.

Peter said to Jesus: "Master, how good it is for us to be here. Let us set up three booths, one for you, one for Moses, and one for Elijah."

While Peter was still speaking, a cloud appeared and overshadowed them. From the cloud came a voice saying, "This is my Son, my chosen one. Listen to him."

Lazarus Emerges from the Tomb

JESUS RAISES LAZARUS FROM THE DEAD

WHEN Lazarus, Jesus' good friend, became very sick, his sisters, Martha and Mary, sent for Jesus. But Jesus stayed where he was for a couple of days because, knowing what he was going to do, he had to allow Lazarus to die.

Lazarus was dead for four days when Jesus arrived in Bethany. The sisters were very upset when they went out to meet him. They wanted to trust in him, but they were filled with sadness.

Jesus went to the tomb and told the people to roll back the stone from the entrance. After praying to the Father, he said, "Lazarus, come out!" Lazarus came back to life. Jesus told those around him to free Lazarus from his burial clothes.

Jesus Enters Jerusalem in Triumph

THE PEOPLE PRAISE JESUS

ONE day Jesus rode into Jerusalem on a donkey. Along the road people spread their cloaks on the ground for him to ride over.

They cut palm branches to wave as he rode by. They shouted the same words that we say every day at Mass: "Blessed is he who comes in the name of the Lord!"

When Jesus entered Jerusalem, the whole city was shaken. Many people heard the noise as the crowd cried out their greeting; so they were asking, "Who is this?"

The disciples of Jesus answered, "This is the prophet from Nazareth in Galilee."

Jesus Prays at the Last Supper

THE LAST SUPPER

ON the night before he died Jesus sat down at supper with his Apostles. During the meal Jesus took some bread, blessed and broke it. Then he gave it to the Apostles, saying: "Take and eat. This is my body."

After the supper, he took a cup. He gave thanks and passed the cup to his Apostles, saying: "Take and drink all of this: for this is my blood which is to be poured out for the forgiveness of sins."

Then he told the Apostles to do what he had just done. And this has continued to be done in his name up to the present time at Mass every day.

Jesus Prays in the Garden of Gethsemane

THE AGONY IN THE GARDEN

JESUS took with him Peter, James, and John, and went into the garden of Gethsemane. He said, "My soul is sad, even unto death. Wait here and watch with me."

He went apart from them and fell down, crying out, "Father, if it is possible, let this cup pass away from me; yet not as I will, but as you will."

Jesus returned to his Apostles and found them asleep. He said, "Could you not watch one hour with me?" He then told them to watch and pray, and he returned to pray to the Father.

Once again, Jesus found them sleeping. He prayed a third time, and an angel came to strengthen him.

Jesus Says He Is a King

JESUS IS CONDEMNED TO DEATH

THE high priest and the court found Jesus guilty, and sent him to the Roman governor for conviction.

Pilate asked Jesus, who stood before him, "Are you the King of the Jews?"

And Jesus replied, "You have said it. I am a King. That is why I was born, and why I have come into the world, to bear witness to the truth."

Pilate presented Jesus to the people. But the crowd kept shouting for Jesus to be put to death. Even though Pilate knew Jesus was innocent, he gave him over to the soldiers to be crucified.

Jesus Dies on the Cross

JESUS DIES ON THE CROSS

THE Roman soldiers laid the Cross on Jesus, and they started for Calvary—the place of the crucifixion.

On the way, Jesus fell under the weight of the Cross and his previous beatings. The soldiers forced a passer-by, Simon of Cyrene, to help him.

On Calvary the soldiers stripped Jesus and nailed him to the Cross. Standing by the Cross were Mary, his Mother, and John, the beloved disciple.

After three hours of terrible pain on the Cross, Jesus said, "It is consummated." And having said this, he expired.

Jesus Rises from the Dead

JESUS RISES FROM THE DEAD

ON three separate occasions Jesus had told his Apostles that he would rise on the third day after his death.

On the Sunday (third day) after his death he rose by his own divine power, a glorious Victor, as he had promised. His body would suffer no more. The prince of life, who died, overcame death and reigns forever.

Jesus appeared to Mary Magdalene, calming her fears that his tomb was empty. He sent her to go to the disciples to proclaim that he had risen from the dead.

The Resurrection of Jesus shows us that he is the Son of God and that if we follow him we too shall one day rise glorious.

The Holy Spirit Comes

THE HOLY SPIRIT COMES

AFTER Jesus had ascended into heaven the disciples were with our Lady. Suddenly they heard a sound from heaven like the noise of a great wind.

They saw tongues of fire, and they were filled with the Holy Spirit. They began to praise God, telling all the people how good God is and how wonderful are all his works. Many of these people came to believe what Peter said that day and came forward to be baptized at Peter's invitation.

The disciples understood, better than ever before, that God loves us and that we must do everything we can to show him that we love him.

DAILY PRAYERS

The Our Father

See p. 39.

The Hail Mary

Hail, Mary, full of grace! The Lord is with thee; blessed art thou among women, and blessed is the fruit of thy womb, Jesus. Holy Mary, mother of God, pray for us sinners, now and at the hour of our death. Amen.

The Glory Be

Glory be to the Father, and to the Son, and to the Holy Spirit. As it was in the beginning, is now, and ever shall be, world without end. Amen.

The Apostles' Creed

I believe in God, the Father almighty, Creator of heaven and earth, and in Jesus Christ, his only Son, our Lord, who was conceived by the Holy Spirit, born of the Virgin Mary, suffered under Pontius Pilate, was crucified, died and was buried; he descended into hell; the third day he arose again from the dead; he ascended into heaven, and is seated at the right hand of God the Father almighty; from there he will come to judge the living and the dead.

I believe in the Holy Spirit, the holy Catholic Church, the Communion of saints, the forgiveness of sins, the resurrection of the body, and life everlasting. Amen.

Act of Faith

O my God, I believe in you, and I believe all that the holy Catholic Church teaches.

Act of Hope

O my God, I hope in you; please forgive my sins and lead me to heaven.

Act of Love

O my God, I love you will all my heart and soul because you are so great and so good.

Act of Contrition

O my God, I am heartily sorry for having offended you and I detest all my sins, because of your just punishments, but most of all because of they offend you, my God, who are all-good and deserving of all my love.

I firmly resolve, with the help of your grace, to sin no more and to avoid the near occasions of sin. Amen.

Morning Prayers

O my God, I believe in you, I hope in you. I love you above all things. I thank you for having brought me safely through this night.

I give my whole self to you. Everything I do today, I will do to please you. Keep me, dear Jesus, from all evil. Bless my father and mother, and all those I love.

Holy Mary, pray for me.

Our Father. Hail Mary.

Evening Prayers

O God, I thank you for the many blessings I have received today. Forgive me all my sins. I am sorry for them all because I have displeased you. Bless me while I sleep so that I may do better tomorrow. Bless my father and mother and all those I love, and make them happy.

Jesus, Mary and Joseph help me, especially in the hour of my death. Amen.

Our Father. Hail Mary.

SACRAMENT OF PENANCE

(CONFESSION)

Jesus knew that even though his example and help would aid us to be better, we would fail him sometimes by sinning. That is why he left us the Sacrament of Penance. In this Sacrament, Jesus comes to forgive our sins and brings peace with God and with the Church, which is hurt by our sins. We must be truly sorry for doing wrong and sincerely try to do better.

Examination of Conscience

Before confessing my sins to a priest so that they may be forgiven, I must tell Jesus how sorry I am and how much I need his help. Then I must try to remember my sins by examining my conscience. Her are some helps:

- Have I tried to understand how necessary God is in my life? Since my last confession how often have I prayed to him, how often have I preferred to ignore him? Why have I done these things?
- Have I been my best at home—toward my parents, my brothers and sisters, my work, my friends? If I have not, why haven't I? I cannot do better unless I try to know why I have done wrong.
- Have I been the best student I can be? Do I pay attention, study hard, do my homework, respect my teachers? Am I kind to other children; do I respect school property? Can I

think of any other way I may not have done my best at school?

- Have I been fair and honest toward my friends when I play, or when I go on trips, or when I'm walking back and forth to school? If not, why haven't I?
- Have I shown respect for my body and taken good care of it?

Prayers before Confession

Jesus, before you died you prayed that you and I would always be united. Do not let me ever do anything to stray away from you. When I sin, take me back as your friend.

O God, I am sorry for all my sins because they are not pleasing to you and you are so good and deserving of all my love. With your help I will sin no more.

How to Make My Confession

1. Make the Sign of the Cross.
2. Tell the priest when I made my last Confession.
3. Confess my sins.
4. Listen to what the priest tells me.
5. Say an Act of Contrition (sorrow).
6. Thank the priest after he has given me absolution in the name of Jesus.

After Confession, I must say the penance the priest gave me. Then I must thank God for forgiving my sins and ask his help to avoid sin in the future.

COMMUNION PRAYERS

BEFORE HOLY COMMUNION

An Act of Offering

Dear Jesus, with this Holy Communion, I offer you today, my thoughts, my words, and all that I do. May your grace help me to be always ready to receive you.

An Act of Faith

O good Jesus, you are now on the altar. I believe that you are the same God who made heaven and earth, and who became a child like me to draw us all close to you. I believe that now you are really present in Holy Communion to be the food of our souls. I believe it all because you said so.

An Act of Hope

O good Jesus, you come to me with the riches of heaven and earth. I truly hope that you will bring me all the help I need to serve you well and to get to heaven.

An Act of Love

Dear Jesus, how much I should love you, after all that you have suffered for me. Make me grow more and more in love for you. How happy I shall be when in a few moments I shall hold you close to my heart.

An Act of Contrition

I know, dear Jesus, I have often offended you by my sins. But I am very sorry now. One word from your holy lips, and my soul will be whiter than snow. I promise, dear Jesus, to be very careful not to offend you again.

An Act of Adoration

My Lord and my God, I believe that you are really present in the Blessed Sacrament. I adore you, O Jesus, my Creator, my Lord, my Redeemer, my Love.

Come, dear Jesus, come into my heart. I am going to receive you in Holy Communion. You are God.

My Lord and my God!

Prayer to Thank Jesus for Coming to Me

Dear Jesus, your miracles are very great. Your greatest miracle is that of giving your body and blood to us in Holy Communion. This is you yourself and not just bread.

I thank you for giving yourself to me. May this Holy Communion bring me closer to you, my Lord and my God.

Acts of Faith, Hope, Love and Petition

O good Jesus, you are king of heaven and earth. I believe in you. I hope in you. I love you.

O Jesus, I have just eaten you as food for my soul. You are God's gift to me to help me imitate you. There are many things I need from you so I may do what you want me to.

Help me especially to love my family, my friends, everyone, as you love them. I forgive anyone who has ever done wrong to me. Help me to love my enemies and do good to everyone, even those who hurt me. Jesus, for you I live; for you I die; I wish to be yours forever.

An Act of Joy

May my soul always want you, O dear Jesus.

May you always be with us in Holy Communion.

May you live in my heart always.

May your many graces help me to be happy with you forever in heaven.

An Act of Offering

O Jesus, you have given yourself to me; now let me give myself to you.

I give you my body, that it may be chaste and pure. I give you my soul, that it may be free from sin. I give you my heart, that it may always love you.

I give you every thought, word, and deed of my life, and I offer all for your honor and glory.